$\mathcal{M}$ay the contents of this book
be a help and a comfort
as you face a difficult decision.

To _____

From _____

Acknowledgments

"Duchess" is reprinted with permission
of the author, Jean Foster.

"My Little Cat Ghost" appeared originally in *Cat
Fancy* and is reprinted with permission
of the author, Lynette Combs.

We have been unable to locate Tony D'Agnese,
author of "Ode to I Ching," and ask that he
or any reader who knows him contact the publisher.

"Where to Bury a Dog" by Ben Hur Lampman is
reprinted with permission of *The Oregonian*.

A Final Act of Caring:
Ending the Life of an Animal Friend

First printing: 1993   Fifth printing: 1999
Second printing: 1995   Sixth printing: 2001
Third printing: 1996   Seventh printing: 2002
Fourth printing: 1998   Eighth printing: 2003

ISBN 1-879779-02-1
Printed in the United States of America

In grateful appreciation to all those
who shared their stories so
that others might benefit
from their experience.

Also a special thank you to
Dr. Tina Ellenbogen, D.V.M.,
Elizabeth Branch of the Delta Society,
Dee Ready and Lea Hall
who read the manuscript
and gave us the benefit
of their expertise.

By the Authors

Other pet-related books

Good-bye My Friend:
Grieving the Loss of a Pet

Your Aging Pet:
Making the Senior Years Healthy and Rewarding

Other grief-related books

Beyond Sorrow:
Christian Reflections on Death and Grief

Into the Light:
How to Pray with the Sick and the Dying
(with Ron DelBene)

A Time to Mourn
(with Ron DelBene)

Contents

When the Bad News Comes

*M*arcia was a young wife and mother when a pup who had gotten the worst of a fight followed her youngest son home from kindergarten. The dog wore no tags, so Marcia's three children just knew he was meant to be theirs. They called him Woofer because of his bark, and that night Marcia fed him table scraps on an old pie tin. By morning the dog with the pleading eyes of a spaniel and the silky coat of a setter had found a place in Marcia's heart. When none of her attempts to find his owner succeeded, Woofer became part of the family.

Over the next fourteen years Marcia experienced many changes in her life. Her father died. Her marriage failed. One by one her children left home. But through it all, Woofer was always there for her; always her one sure source of comfort. Then came the dreadful news: Woofer had a liver disease for which there was no cure.

At first Marcia denied the diagnosis. She was sure that with medication and a lot of TLC, Woofer would get better. But attentive as she was, and hard as Woofer struggled to hang on, his condition worsened. He could no longer catch a Frisbee or interact in other playful ways. Even slow walks with Marcia tired him.

The veterinarian did not think Woofer was in much physical pain, but the day came when Marcia could no longer deny the sorrowful, defeated look in his eyes. That night she called her children. Each agreed that the time had come to let Woofer be free of the prison his body had become.

Sometimes a decision about euthanasia has to be made immediately, but often this is not the case. Like Marcia, you probably have time to discuss options with your veterinarian and talk about your feelings with family and friends.

Heartbreaking as it is to get a bleak diagnosis, an anticipated death may be easier to cope with than one that is unexpected. When death comes without warning, there is no time to absorb the shock or reflect on decisions that must be made. With even a little time on your side, you have an opportunity to say your good-byes and do what you think is best for your animal friend—a friend who enriched your life so greatly and who will be so profoundly missed.

JUDY J. KING

Anticipatory Grief

When Marcia learned that Woofer's liver disease was fatal, she began experiencing anticipatory grief. Unlike grief after a loss that becomes less intense over time, anticipatory grief becomes more intense as the loss approaches.

Like Marcia, Nancy also found that her grief began with the diagnosis. "I act okay in front of other people—even my husband and 14-year-old son," she said two months after her treasured calico had been diagnosed with leukemia. "But when I'm alone I feel like I'm falling apart. Every night I cry myself to sleep. As the days pass, I feel worse and worse. If I'm like this now, I can't imagine how I'll feel when the end comes."

While anticipatory grief may shorten the period of grieving after the loss, it becomes a problem if the loss is delayed too long. Grief that intensifies over time interferes with the ability to be rational. A grieving pet owner who is unable to make clearheaded decisions might force an animal into a painfully prolonged life.

One of the characteristics of grief is a feeling of helplessness. It's not surprising then that pet owners experiencing anticipatory grief often want their veterinarian to decide when the time to euthanize has come. But making that decision is not the veterinarian's role. Even though your vet might suggest euthanasia as the most caring option, the decision is up to you. What you can expect your vet to provide is information and guidance regarding your pet's changing condition and status. You can also expect compassionate understanding of what you are going through.

Although a humane death will end your pet's suffering, it may be just the beginning of your own emotional pain. Speak with your veterinarian and others knowledgeable about support services in your area. Making use of these services along with the resources listed in the last section of this book will help you face your decision and deal with your grief both before and after your loss.

Facing the Decision

*I*n order to make a sound decision, you need to be fully informed about your pet's condition and the medical options available. If any part of the diagnosis or its implications for your pet's future is unclear, ask for a further explanation. You may want a second opinion to assure yourself that the diagnosis is correct, and that you have all the facts. But even with the facts in hand, it is often difficult to know just when the time has come.

Brandy had been deeply attached to Frank's wife, and after her death the splendid Persian transferred her affection to Frank. Over the next four years each was nurtured by what the other had to give. But then Brandy was diagnosed as having an inoperable tumor, and day by day Frank saw her life ebbing away. Even though his mind told him that euthanizing Brandy was the right thing to do, his heart kept holding him back.

"The really hard part was deciding which day would be her last," said Frank. "Every evening I'd think, *If I'd had her put down today, she wouldn't be curled up in my lap tonight.*" Only when Brandy stopped eating and meowed in pain whenever Frank picked her up was he able to make the decision he'd been avoiding.

When facing your own decision, a home visit by your veterinarian may be helpful. Your pet can then be assessed at his or her best in familiar surroundings rather than in a hospital setting. A veterinarian who does not make house calls may be able to collaborate with one who does. In preparation for the home visit, the two vets would work together to have a complete medical background. They might also be able to provide home hospice care as well as home euthanasia if that is desired and feasible. To learn more about these possibilities, consult your veterinarian or local veterinary association.

Frank's cat had been regularly treated by a veterinarian who made housecalls. Thus when Frank decided it was time to end Brandy's life, he had her euthanized at home where she had always been cared for and loved. Afterward Frank wrapped Brandy in the blanket that had lined her basket and entrusted her body to the veterinarian. In a prior consultation with the vet, Frank had decided to have Brandy cremated and her ashes returned to him.

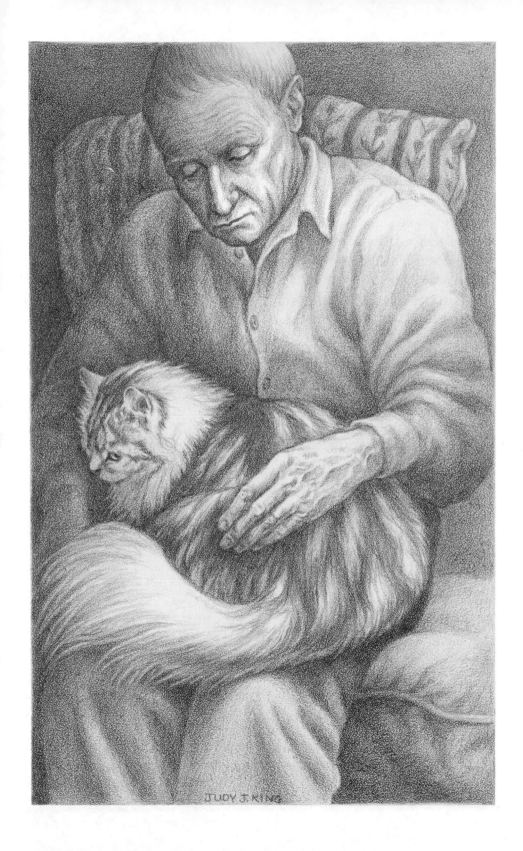

JUDY J. KING

Questions to Ask Yourself

*M*aking the decision to euthanize is often harder than dealing with the loss itself. Many people say they can accept the death and accompanying sadness, but have great difficulty with being the one who must decide when death will occur. Janice, whose 14-year-old dachshund was in steadily declining health, said, "Each night I pray that when I wake up in the morning I'll find that Buster died in his sleep. That way I won't have to make the decision I've been dreading."

Janice's admission reflects what many people feel as their animal companions struggle against all odds. As you face the painful decision about euthanizing your pet, let the following questions serve as your guide:

- Is there a reasonable chance for a cure? for comfort?
- How much additional time might treatment give? What will the quality of that time be?
- Do I have the financial and emotional resources to handle long-term medical care if it is required?
- Will I have the necessary physical and emotional stamina? (Getting up at night, preparing special food, giving shots ...)
- Is the relationship with my pet changing or decreasing in quality as I anticipate this loss?
- How many of my pet's usual activities are still possible? Make a list and review it on a regular basis.
- Is my pet suffering even though physical pain is not evident?
- What do I think my pet would want ?
- If I were in my pet's place, what would I want?
- What is my personal bottom line—what am I unable to tolerate and/or live with? Write a contract with yourself, knowing that you can always renegotiate.
- Project yourself ahead in time and ask, "How will I look back and remember this experience?"

When a pet is suffering or has a severely diminished quality of life and you decide to euthanize, you are doing what you believe is best for your animal friend. Let that thought remain uppermost in your mind as you face your decision, and again as you look back on the action you took.

Duchess

December 28, 1970 to September 6, 1984

I was young!
I ran like the wind and
The world glistened, fresh and new
With each season.
Colorful leaves raced across the lawn,
Crisp and elusive.
Snowflakes danced in howling winds,
But winter posed no threat.
I was young!
Each season blended into the next,
And each displayed its beauty.
The years passed.
Your joys were mine, as were your sorrows;
Our love grew in understanding and
I served you faithfully.
Now, out of your love for me
I ask your courage.
I am old!
My sight has dimmed.
I no longer greet each season with joy.
I cannot run and my body knows pain.
So have the wisdom, dear friend, out of love,
To bid me farewell, and send me on my way
With dignity.
And cherish each season that we shared,
For they are eternity.

Jean Foster

A Gentle and Humane End

*D*iscuss with your veterinarian where the euthanasia will be performed and the best time to do it. Most often it is done in a clinic or animal hospital, but some veterinarians come to the home. If you need reassurance that you are making the right decision, ask for one last review of the situation and your options.

The euthanasia procedure is accomplished by injecting a special solution similar to a concentrated anesthesia drug into a vein. Other routes are possible depending upon the personality and medical status of the animal. Sometimes an intravenous catheter will be placed to ensure access to the vein. The animal may—but does not always—feel the needle being inserted. The drug causes a deep sleep after which the breathing center and heart stop. This usually occurs within 30 to 60 seconds, but may take slightly longer for some very old or chronically ill animals.

Your pet can detect your emotional state, so be present only if you are able to provide calm support. Some people realize that witnessing the procedure would be too distressing and decide not to be there. Others take comfort in seeing death come gently and quickly, especially if the animal is suffering.

"As I drove Koko to the vet, my heart was breaking," said Coralee. "Still I was determined to be with her to the end. As she lay on the table in the vet's office I held her head between my hands and told her of my love. Even though she was terribly weak, she raised her head one last time and gave me a lingering, soulful look. I'm positive it was her way of saying, *'Thank you for letting me go.'*"

If you choose not to be present, don't feel guilty. Veterinarians and their staffs are dedicated to seeing that the final moments of an animal's life are as peaceful and painless as possible. The last thing your pet will know is the sound of a kindly voice and the touch of caring, competent hands. You may want to spend time with your pet before the procedure or say a final good-bye afterward. Seeing the body one last time provides closure. It may also help assure you that your pet is at peace and that euthanasia was the correct decision.

My Little Cat Ghost

The years I've worn you,
warm upon my shoulder,
ended here...
surprised to find us older.

And there was nothing
left to do today
but hold you close
and help you on your way.

Be still, my little cat.
Be well; be free.
I know that you're somewhere near,
and loving me.

Lynette Combs

JUDY J. KING

What to Do with the Body

*E*veryone who loses an animal to death must decide what to do with the body. Some people leave the body with their veterinarian who determines what will be done with it. Others consult with their veterinarian about the options available and then come to a decision.

Sally and the cat with whom she shared her life for an all-too-brief eleven months started saying their good-byes the day Agate was diagnosed with a terminal illness. Six weeks later on a sunny July morning, Sally asked the vet to free Agate from her pain.

Afterward Sally brought her cat's body home. With the help and comfort of a friend, she buried Agate in the day lily patch behind the garage. This simple, tender burial was something Sally had been planning since the day the vet told her that medically there was nothing more he could do to help Agate.

Home Burial. Like Sally, many people bury their pets on their own property or that of friends or relatives. (Check with your veterinarian or municipal government to see if this is permitted in your area.) To guard against the remains being unearthed by children or animals, a grave should be a minimum of three feet deep. A box or special holder is sometimes required, and will protect the remains. Burial items can be purchased from a funeral director or pet cemetery. Many pet owners make a casket themselves or creatively decorate a suitable box.

Cemetery Burial. There are more than 500 pet cemeteries in the United States, with every state having at least one. The plot, casket and marker usually carry separate fees. A charge might also be made for digging the grave.

An official pet cemetery—as opposed to an animal burial ground—is on "dedicated land." This means that no matter who owns the land, it will always remain a cemetery. A pet cemetery must meet standards set by the International Association of Pet Cemeteries. A list of cemeteries (both US and Canadian) is available free of charge from IAPC, 13 Cemetery Lane, Box 163, Ellenburg Depot, NY 12935. Telephone (800) 952-5541. Include a business-size, self-addressed stamped envelope with your written request.

Community Services. Some communities have a free pet euthanasia service. Some also offer free pickup of the remains when an animal dies at home. Check with your city hall for information.

Communal Burial. This option is offered by some pet cemeteries and humane societies and is less costly than a private burial.

Cremation. Many people choose to have their pets cremated, which is often a practical alternative to burial. Some veterinary clinics have their own crematoriums, as do many pet cemeteries and humane organizations. Veterinarians who do not have these facilities arrange to have the cremation done elsewhere.

Communal Cremation. Cremating more than one animal at a time is a common practice and costs less than an individual cremation. When making the decision to cremate, it's important to specify whether you want an individual or a communal cremation.

Animal ashes can be dealt with in various ways. Many people like to scatter them; in doing so they feel they are releasing their pet's body and spirit to the earth and sky. Woods or an open field are popular places for scattering ashes. So, too, are beds of flowers whose beauty symbolizes the owner's relationship with the pet. (Before scattering ashes, check with your veterinarian or municipal government to see what regulations apply in your area.)

Other options for dealing with ashes are storing them in an urn or burying them. One bereaved pet owner put her cat's ashes in a glass jar and included favorite playthings. She then decorated the jar with ribbons and buried it between the two peony bushes where her cat loved to doze on hot summer afternoons.

There is no single right way to deal with an animal's remains. Whatever is respectful, whatever brings a measure of comfort and closure to your life together is the appropriate thing to do.

Where to Bury a Dog

…there is one place that is best of all.
If you bury him in this spot,
the secret of which you must already have,
he will come to you when you call—
come to you over the grim, dim frontiers of death,
and down the well-remembered path,
and to your side again.
And though you call a dozen living dogs to heel
they shall not growl at him, nor resent his coming,
for he is yours and he belongs there.

People may scoff at you,
who see no lightest blade of grass bent by his footfall,
who hear no whimper pitched too fine for audition,
people who may never really have had a dog.
Smile at them, for you shall know something
that is hidden from them,
and which is well worth the knowing.
The best place to bury a dog
is in the heart of his master.

Ben Hur Lampman

Paying Last Respects

*B*ecause society has no formal rite for laying a beloved pet to rest, we need to create our own rituals. For some people it is ritual enough to have a few moments of respectful silence or to reverently hang the pet's leash behind the kitchen door one last time. But others feel a need to do something more.

"In our family we honor all the important passages with rituals," said Bill. "It starts with christenings and ends with funerals. So when we had to euthanize our faithful old dog Rocky, it was important to mark his passing."

Bill recalled how on a golden September afternoon his family and a few friends gathered at Rocky's grave. "We stood in a circle and my daughter Katie read a poem she'd written for the occasion. Then we took turns sharing memories of Rocky. To end our little ceremony we joined hands and I said a prayer of gratitude for all the ways Rocky had enriched our lives."

How you choose to honor your pet will be as individual as the relationship you shared. Following are ways others have dignified the passing of a cherished animal:

- Take a day off work. If you need a reason, tell the truth: say, "My best friend died."
- Write a eulogy describing what your pet meant to you.
- Compose a poem or write a song about your pet.
- Compile a scrapbook or photo album.
- Display a picture of your pet and burn a votive candle beside it during your most intense mourning.
- Notify friends who will understand and be supportive.
- Observe Pet Memorial Day on the second Sunday in September.
- Make a donation to a charity organization in memory of your pet.

JUDY J. KING

Children and Pet Loss

"Some of my happiest childhood memories include a dog named Gracie," said Ellen. "But one day when I came home from school, she didn't run down the walk to greet me. And when I went to bed that night, she still hadn't come home. The next day my mother said that Gracie must have run away, which bothered me terribly. *Was it because I hadn't played with her enough?* I worried. *Or because I got crabby and pushed her away sometimes?*"

Ellen searched tirelessly for her dog—a search that finally ended the day she found Gracie's collar in the basement. When Ellen showed the collar to her parents, they admitted that they'd taken Gracie to the vet. Because the dog was old and sick and couldn't get well, the vet ended her life. "I was heartbroken that I'd never see Gracie again," Ellen said. "But what made the pain even worse was that my parents hadn't told me the truth. If they had, I would've been able to say good-bye."

Ellen put the collar that still smelled of the dog in a paper bag and kept it in her room. "Whenever I felt lonesome for Gracie," she said, "I'd open the bag and take a deep breath."

To help children cope with the loss of a pet, it's useful to know how they view death at various ages. Up to about age five, children don't realize that death is permanent—you're dead for a time, then pop back to life. Somewhere between five and nine children understand the permanence of death, but aren't convinced that it comes to all living things. Around age ten children have the emotional and mental capacity to understand the finality of death.

After a family pet dies, children may experience the same sorrow as an adult but express their feelings differently. Immediately following the death children are likely to be so overwhelmed by the loss that they are not yet able to grieve. No matter how children deal with their loss, they need understanding and reassurance that there will always be someone to care for them.

Although it may be tempting to quickly get another pet, this is generally not a good idea. Children need to understand that each life is unique and irreplaceable. If they see that a much-loved pet is easily replaced, they may worry that they are replaceable as well.

Guidelines for Helping Children

- Review the veterinarian's report with your family. If treatment would be an emotional or financial burden, discuss this openly.

- Explain that your pet's condition is nobody's fault. Children may think they are responsible because they failed to walk the dog or keep the cat's water dish filled.

- Be forthright about your own feelings and what the loss of the family pet will mean to you. This encourages children to be open and honest as well.

- Never try to protect children by making up stories. If they later learn the facts, they may think, *My parents didn't tell the truth about this, so what else have they lied to me about?*

- Explain that euthanasia is a quick, gentle death. The animal becomes unconscious, and then the breathing and heart stop.

- Do not refer to euthanasia as "putting an animal to sleep." Children may fear that if they fall asleep they, too, might die.

- Encourage children to find creative outlets for their feelings: write stories, poems, songs or make a scrapbook in memory of their pet.

- Discuss what will be done with the animal's body. This helps children confront the reality of death and lets them feel involved in important family decisions.

- Give children an opportunity to say their good-byes.

- Talk about how fortunate your family has been to have such a special pet, and how nothing can take away the memories. They will be yours forever.

JUDY J. KING

JUDY J. KING

Saying Good-bye

*C*harles believed that every child should grow up with a dog, so shortly after his first son, Cody, was born he brought one home. She was an Irish setter puppy that Charles and his wife named Spicer. In the years that followed, another son and a daughter joined the family. Spicer endeared herself to them as well. For each of the children she was a playmate, an ally and always someone to talk to when no one else understood their hurts and disappointments. To the grown-ups she was the eternal child who never passed judgment and loved them as much on their good days as their bad.

For sixteen years Spicer led a full and active life. After that, age was no longer kind to her: cataracts dimmed her sight. Her hearing failed. Her joints stiffened. When even getting up became a painful effort, the family gathered to discuss what they all knew needed to be done. But before they could let Spicer go to a gentle death, they needed to say their good-byes.

Everyone gave Spicer extra attention. They talked to her, and groomed her, and made sure she got her favorite foods. Whenever she showed an interest in going outside, someone was always ready to take her for a slow walk along familiar paths.

On Spicer's last day the family gathered for a photo. As usual Spicer was in the center, still managing to look regal. Afterward each member of the family had time alone with Spicer: time to stroke her fur, hug her and say a final farewell. Friends also came by to lovingly send Spicer on her way.

Finding ways to say good-bye is an important step in managing the sorrow that naturally accompanies the loss of an animal friend. Even though it's painful to see death coming, knowing the end is near gives you the opportunity to take those last caring actions that say to your pet, *You have always been safest in my care.*

Other Pets

*O*o animals grieve? Many people believe they do. Knowing how some surviving pets have reacted to loss prepares you for experiences you may have.

Hank and Lilli were prized Afghans, and Hank—the older of the pair—relished being Lilli's protector and role model. The two were inseparable until a sudden illness took Hank's life. Lilli reacted by curling up on the floor. For three days she refused to eat or drink, and quickly lost muscle tone. Even when her owners snuggled beside her and spoke soothingly, she failed to respond.

A turning point came when guests coaxed Lilli outside for a walk on a beautiful spring day. As she stepped into the sunshine and stopped to sniff along the road, her interest in life was obviously returning. But Lilli didn't come fully alive until the family acquired a greyhound who had exhausted his usefulness at a nearby racetrack. With this new, younger dog in the house, Lilli assumed Hank's role of senior partner and both animals thrived.

Individual animals have their own way of reacting to loss. Marta and Mario had been companions since they were kittens. When Mario died, Marta refused to eat. Listlessness took over. No matter how much attention she was given, she remained indifferent to everyone and everything around her. This behavior continued until the day Mario's ashes were brought home. Then, standing in front of the china cabinet where the ashes had been placed, Marta gave one long, piteous yowl. After that she resumed eating and again became the contented cat she had always been.

Yowling or whimpering, listlessness, a refusal to eat or drink are some behaviors you might observe. A previously affectionate animal may avoid you, or even be hostile. Try to be patient and understanding. Speak to surviving pets often and be generous with affection. To alleviate loneliness when you're away, leave the TV on or play a radio softly. Something major is missing both from your life and from that of the surviving animal. Together you are experiencing the pain of loss.

JUDY J. KING

Finding the Support You Need

*G*rief is the natural reaction to loss. The death of a beloved pet can be even more painful than the loss of a person who has played a significant part in your life. But because the love-tie that exists between animals and humans is not yet widely appreciated, there is a stigma attached to grieving for a pet. "It was only a dog," unknowing people will say. Or, "You can always get another cat." What these people fail to understand is that you are not grieving for just any animal. Your grief is for a unique and irreplaceable friend with whom you shared a deeply personal relationship on a daily basis

"To me Sherlock was the most special dog in the whole world," said Evelyn, whose Pomeranian would have been 20 on his next birthday. "Between the time his cancer was diagnosed and the day I asked the vet to end his suffering, I thought I'd done most of my grieving. *What a surprise I was in for!* After Sherlock was gone, sorrow rolled over me in such giant waves I thought I would drown in it. If I'd known what help was available to me, I'd have reached out sooner."

At first you may need to come to terms with a devastating diagnosis or take time to absorb the finality of the death and mourn in private. But the most difficult grief is that which is borne alone. If you are willing to reach out for help, your pain will be easier to bear.

Your veterinarian. Immediately after the euthanasia, or in the next day or two, ask for a consultation if you feel the need for one. Either talk on the phone or schedule an office visit. Veterinarians cannot be expected to be professionally certified grief counselors, but they are in a position to be sensitive to your pain. They can answer questions, offer reassurance about your decision to euthanize and be a resource for further information and support. If a consultation is too painful, or for the time being you are too emotional to speak, send your veterinarian a note and ask to be called back.

An understanding friend or acquaintance. This needs to be someone to whom you can pour out your heart and know that you will be listened to and understood.

A pet loss support group. Members of pet loss support groups have either lost a pet or are facing a decision about euthanasia. One of the more troubling questions surrounding euthanasia is, *When is the right time?* Although the answer differs with each situation, others who have anguished over the same question are best able to be supportive. Through sharing their stories of loss, grieving pet owners help both themselves and one another. If there is no support group in your area, you may want to start one.

One-on-one therapy. Increasingly, grieving pet owners are turning to professional therapists for help in dealing with their loss. Consult your veterinarian, local humane society or the Delta Society for guidance in locating a qualified therapist in your area.

Delta Society. This nonprofit membership organization located in Renton, Washington, is the leading information center on people and animal interactions. Materials offered include a bibliography of publications on pet loss for both children and adults, videotapes on pet loss and bereavement, the National Directory of Pet Loss Counselors and a listing of pet loss support groups and hotline numbers throughout the country. The Delta Society can be reached by phone at 425-226-7357or by e-mail at info@deltasociety.org. Their website is www.deltasociety.org.

Pet loss hotlines. Support for grieving pet owners is available by phone. One pet loss hotline is operated by veterinary students at the University of California–Davis. This free service handles only incoming calls and cannot return long-distance calls. The number is (916) 752-4200 and is answered Monday through Friday from 6:30 P.M. to 9:30 P.M. PST. (For other hotline numbers contact the Delta Society.)

Good-bye My Friend. This book offers consolation at the time of death and sustains the bereaved pet owner with understanding and reassurance throughout the grieving period. *Good-bye My Friend* is by the authors of *A Final Act of Caring.* To order a single copy of either book, send $5.95 (or $9.20 for two)—includes postage and handling—to Montgomery Press, PO Box 24124, Minneapolis, MN 55424.

Ode to I Ching

Close your eyes now,
my longtime friend,
and let this
time of suffering
come to a peaceful end.
We'll walk together
soon, I'm sure,
as winter turns to spring,
when snow gives way
to budding leaves
and birds begin to sing.
The gentle breeze
shall call your name
along the water's edge.
For what we shared
and what you meant
shall never be forgot.
Your friendship spans
the years behind
your memory ahead.
You'll always be
there next to me,
companion and good friend.

Tony D'Agnese